Semidomesticated

Jonie McIntire

The first limited edition of this text appeared from
Red Flag Poetry in 2021

ISBN: 979-8-9855242-2-2

Sheila-Na-Gig Editions
Russell, KY
Hayley Mitchell Haugen, Editor
www.sheilanagigblog.com

ACKNOWLEDGMENTS

Special note to acknowledge poems previously published:

Dissonance Magazine: "On Taking Chewable Acidophilous"
Gasconade Review: "On Driving Heather to Radiation"
Gasconade Review: Ladies Night: "Grand Island, NE, " "Passage of
    the Divine Bird, Print on My Therapist's Wall"
Gasconade Review: Missouri is a Ghost Shaped Thing: "August
    Prep," "Passing"
Khroma: Home: "The Body of My House"
Khroma, Vol. 2:4: "The Devil Loves Arithmetic"
Museum of Poetry: "Ivory"
North of Oxford: "Easter Sunday for Cynics"
Red Fez: "Diving for Coins," "There's No Easy Way to Patch"
WomenSpeak: "Vinegar for Flies "

This collection is dedicated to pushy women and patient men.
And all the beasts in between.

Contents

The Devil Loves Arithmetic

My love, you should know
that I have already calculated
the life insurance if you died.

The partial disability, your
school loan dissolved, the
extra closet space and shoes

near the door, an extra hook
for coats. And before you bristle,
know this – it has nothing to do

with socks perpetually scattered
on the floor, or the water glass
forever dirty and in the sink.

It's just... the math of it all.
The ease with which lives translate
to numbers and numbers fit

so tidy in boxes and spreadsheets
make stacking boxes easy.
Watching early morning news,

another bombing in a foreign land
where bodies that aren't ours
aren't counted, followed by

a school levy translated to
costs per child and call in to talk —
do you think it's worth paying more?

I can hear you rising
from bed to bath and slow
down stairs, and I can't

help myself – six, seven, board creak
eight. Maybe twenty-three more
until you reach me.

August Prep

Four crates of tomatoes
grace the late August kitchen.

My muscles still jump from
hauling them when I find

Rob has died of cancer,
his young wife and two kids

sending messages they've had
years to rehearse.

In the massive saucepot, we've gathered
lids, bands, funnel, rack

flats of jars create a glass layer
in the trunk of the car and

we are carrying them slowly
into Annette's kitchen

and for a moment, the air
smells of death and tomatoes.

But the pot of water is already boiling
on the stove, and next to it

a bowl of ice and water and the perfect
paring knives we picked

when we did this last year,
and we all begin – hot, then cold,

then peel back the skin and core.
It's the only way to get it all done.

Vinegar for Flies

My grandmother recommended sugar
to impress the church-clad lavender ladies,
the neighborhood scout leaders.
Better than vinegar, though as soon as
doors closed she was drywall-shaking
loud, from foot to throat.

My grandfather, oldest son and academic,
didn't need it. He knew how to hold favor —
by directing, by keeping up the good show,
by lining the smart children in front,
the dull in back or not at all.

My grandmother of bad feet and soft biscuits
wanted to go to college to become a nurse,
but my grandfather insisted.
Too many children already,
too much house to care for.
And too stupid, after all.

Even after twenty years of marriage,
I struggle to show love. Instead,
bake pans of brownies late August,
the kitchen a spatter of flour and jars
of apple cider vinegar, fruit flies
trapped under film, struggling to get out.

On Taking Chewable Acidophilus

My therapist agrees with my general practitioner:
stop drinking beer and eating crap
and start taking your health seriously.

In therapy, I get worksheets about
cognitive behavioral psychology,
filling out emotional inventories every visit.
I start on them like Cosmo questionnaires,
like I'll find out if I'm a spring
or maybe really an autumn
and that vertical stripes
are the trick to feeling beautiful.

But these questions reach
down through the throat,
to old stories I stopped letting myself hear.
To stories I built myself upon. And I realize
this is more than just paperwork.

Diving for Coins

His graduation cap hanging
from a nail on the back of his bedroom door
falls off every time he shuts it fast.
So he has to slow. Says he's not ready
to learn how to drive, to go to work.
Wants one last summer, then start college
but focus on classes. Says "I know" and
"I'll get there" to each reminder.
Only 18, still a kid, really.
As we load up to visit a friend's pool,
he drags feet, complains about sun,
and even with the water light blue clear,
a quarter flung in instead of a penny,
he feels everywhere and takes so
long to come back up.

Blue Light

She wasn't good with the locks
said she always had to call one of the drivers
to get to the boxes on the truck.

This was my first day, first job back home
for summer from university —
Kmart, just to pick up hours.

It was a hook lock on a pivot.
Pull this back, flip that here and you could
use a thick strap to throw the door up and open.

She had already shown me how to fuss over
the toiletries and paper goods, to spin everything
forward, label out – customers like it pretty.

As assistant manager, she got a dollar more
and had waited five years to get here.
By the time we got to the truck, I already knew

about her kids, how the old manager kept
stealing and no one believed her until
he got caught on tape and now that extra dollar

sure makes lay away easier because she's
already socking it, didn't tell a soul - paying
cash for that Playstation for Christmas.

As I worked the lock on yet another truck,
she stood back and studied me - said damn,
don't doors just fly open for you.

And sure as shit, they all did.

Feeder Fish

Waiting for the man at the pet store
to pour crickets into a plastic bag
for an albino leopard gecko hungry
at home, a boy watches goldfish
swimming their circles,
as shoppers wander the pet store,
some rushing to work or home,
some staring slow and mindless
at ferrets, bottom feeders, bearded
dragons and a cockatiel
who will not stop talking.

The feeder fish in the tank
are not all the orange of
goldfish. Some are all white,
or dark face, dark tail.
The boy watches a few
he thinks are prettiest,
the way their fins fan out
like smoke or morning clouds.

But the man with the crickets
shoves the bag into the boy's hand,
scurries over to the tank where
people are circling
and he scoops into the heart
of everything, running the bag
on top of the water
to catch a puddle, then
pouring ten fish in,
eleven cents each, or
ten for a dollar.

Errors in Both Service and Reception

As part of my promotion,
my boss makes me read his favorite
books on business leadership.
To stay sane, I play sand volleyball
at a dive bar near a hospital, three nights
a week, three different teams.

Monday night is killer — two
players are not strong and I've found
the rest of the team shuns them.
My inability to set well has been
the subject of whispers and our top
spiker hits into the net but has reasons.

Thursday night we drink, knock balls
out into parking lot and laugh. Sometimes
nobody hits the ball at all. The other teams
enjoy us, mostly because they win,
but they stay late or show up early just
to practice a bit, joke and show off.

Tuesday is so competitive we are down
to only four players. Those are my
best nights. Ball in the air, there's
no one else to get it for you so you
run. The other team knows when I'm
weak and targets me, so I get better

at returns, at popping the ball straight up
to a teammate. One time, in a weekly
one-on-one meeting with my boss,
when he quizzed me about the books,
I tried to explain to him — how when
the ball is in the air, if nobody calls it

it's yours to hit, that leaders know this.
But that good leaders know when
not to hit as well, when to let the ball fall,
when to let the weaker players try and
fail because otherwise they never get better.
But he just rattled on about *groundswells*

of support and *continually adding value,*
getting to yes and *knowing your role*
in the marketplace. That I needed to know
the ins and outs of coding, data warehousing,
statistical analysis. *Always be the smartest*
person in the room. There's a sound

when the ball hits the sand and everyone
who didn't quite get there looks at the divot,
an awkward silence like recrimination
that turns to pointed fingers and sits like deadweight.
A whole office building can sound like that.
A whole seventeen years.

Easter Sunday for Cynics

When churches weren't open
or her legs too brittle to hold,
my grandmother would watch
on tv, read from pamphlets, reread
old passages in a tattered bible.

She found God every time,
from Jerry Falwell to
the cartoons of the Latter day
Saints to the sun on her back porch.

I wake early, Easter Sunday in a
cynic's house during dark times,
and I check on the robin's nest
tucked away in a second-story
corner window ledge.

Three days ago, just mud and straw.
Then one egg within a day,
two in another. Now,
three perfect eggs more beautiful
than sky or sea.

On the Constant Itching Around Craig's Pain Pump

After shamelessly crushing me at chess, Craig
uses his stronger leg to push himself away
and roll out into the atrium of the art museum.
It's the first time he's been here all year.
His fancy motorized wheelchair doesn't arrive
for another month and he's had this manual one
so long he knows its every hitch and halt.
I put the board away and join him, heading
toward the modern art collection,
where he's lingering in the doorway,
an elderly guard tipping his head to a passing
couple, *Sir, Ma'am. Remember no flash photos.*
The guard hitches for a moment, as if Craig might
run into him and calls out *Hey, looking good there,*
Big Guy, and on seeing me join Craig, *Oooh,*
you got your lady friend, alright Big Guy, there you go!
Craig laughs and we move on to walls of abstractions.
He's unfazed but I can't shake the strangeness.
Craig, don't you think that was weird? You're
a grown man, not a twelve year old. To which Craig
laughs again, shrugs tired shoulders and says
yeah, I'm used to it – whatever. He means well.

Passing

The day my uncle hanged himself in the backyard,
his sister sunbathing in the front, and his brother
spotting him just before the snap,
my father and I toured a college campus,
ate Ethiopian food with our fingers –
my father, always so tidy, humming
as sauce dripped, his pressed grey slacks
wrinkling as he sat cross-legged at a table
on the floor, beaded pillows framing his back.

We drove home listening to hair bands on the radio,
naming the guitarists – he's got the blues guys
but I always beat him in hard rock.
As I watched out the window, surrounded by the steady
turn of tires, my head against the headrest,
I would try to catch the poplars on the roadside –
to see them clearly before they blurred back
into streaky watercolor landscape.
I had to focus, block out everything else
and stare at the tree – pick a leaf and watch
around it, but only for a moment.

Then I lost it and the car seemed faster,
the ground whirring by.
When we got home, it was my mother who told us,
her usually booming voice a small quiet thing,
completely calm.

Ivory

When she washed her hands,
it was a struggle of smells.

Simple soaps like Ivory
to combat the sweaty nickel

scent of fingers, that smell
like desperate midnight breath

his hand over her mouth,
over her nose, the tin

dirt of him feeling
for his lost heart with

dirty fingernails in the
cavity of her eighth year.

Simple soaps so that after
she washed her hands

she could pretend
all of her smelled so clean.

The Muse

Oh muse, I cannot keep dressing these wounds for you.
You hand me a beer, say
sit down, the kids have just now
shut up and maybe they sleep.
Your palm is on the cushion of the couch –
you'd goose me then run off giggling.

Hand me another beer.
Tell me about some other woman
who doesn't whine so much, skinny
and smiling, looks just so,
calls you back when you leave a message.

For you, I am dirt in the air – a reason to spit.
Oh muse, I pickle my liver to bury it with you.
I reach and catch the waist of your pants – pull.
You giggle and swat at my hands.
My fingers are the fattest meat hooks.

Everything slips and only
sweat from the beer can
makes stains on the paper.

Moist

For some,
a terribly awkward
word to pronounce

the roundness of it
the near pucker,
the tongue offered up

like a hunger, like
sex we crave but
love in dreams

is so far different
from love in life,
the odd flood of

orgasm during rape
makes a body
turn itself out

sets its desire in
among guards
among crowns

of tears if actual
desire reaches deep
enough to near it,

there all of the battles
rest, lining the vaginal wall
wanting tense

release, wanting the round
of a wet word, waiting
tongue hesitant

for absolution of
sins a body didn't commit
but sheltered

like someone else's
child, pain in a
womb awaiting

birth but terrified
at every push, at every
honest loving touch.

Writer's Confession

I am the worst kind of cheat.
Sincerely, a thief.
A snitch.
A two-face for sure.
I sleep during work.
I never show up
for the union meetings.
I lost the manual.
My notebook has forgotten
the color of my eyes.
My shoes articulate more
than my fingers.
I lost my best writing pen
in my hair one day
and did nothing but laugh.
I barely read.
I retain nothing, I study
nothing.
I edit feverishly
other people's work.
I write on my
husband's back,
in the condensation
on beer cans,
on prepaid envelopes
with credit card forms
neatly folded inside them.
I am flippant
about prose, about meter,
literary terms and devices.
When you ask me
what am I working on,
nothing.
Every time, nothing.

But you still ask,
and every time
forgive me.
Please,
forgive me.

Grand Island, NE

The wind hisses
at the metal skin of our house,
throws knives so sharp
the dogs line themselves along
my legs, twitching as they dream.

Piled on us,
comforter, afghan, afghan
ripple over us like sandhills.

Under our blankets we are fresh sweat,
listening to Eric Clapton
slowhand as January throws its tantrum,
as fog hovers at power lines, frosts
the insides of windows.

We sleep and radiate.

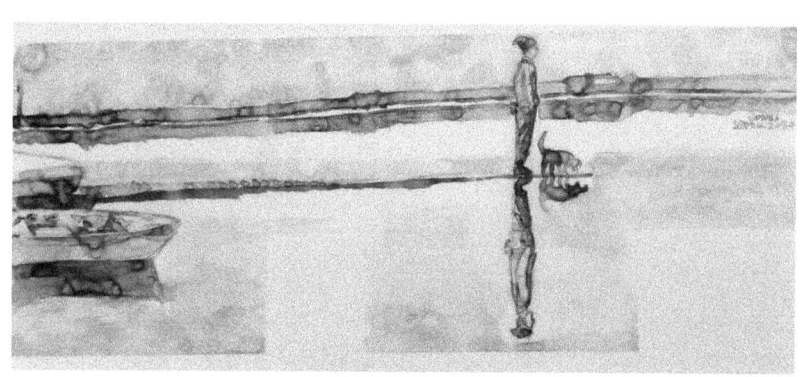

On Driving Heather to Radiation

We're at the clinic just in time to watch Price is Right,
to check out contestants with customized t-shirts
assaulting Drew Carey, shaking and falling like clowns at his feet.

Six weeks of this.

There's free coffee but it's barely beige.
All of the magazines are about cancer except for two.
The Woman's Day from an earlier season
has been memorized by the end of week one
and we joke about writing something silly for Field and Stream,
a camping trip for women who could not care less about nature.

By week three, her hair is falling out but only in the front.
Heather's wearing Steve Tyler scarves and really rocking them.
Shaving her head is the next step, but she's not ready.

As I wait for her, I watch Drew Carey call a housewife from Pasadena
into play and what looks like her entire neighborhood
stands up screaming with joy. And I could swear, if Carey called me up,
I would play and scream and cry just like the people on tv.
I would find the highest bid and add one,
would look to Heather in the crowd reading her face
to decide if the coffee-brewing alarm clock is worth more
than the Liquid X Ultimate car detailing kit.
And the final spin, at the big upright wheel
that's all chance and small flags, big numbers you want
but little that can add up, I'd pray to the god I long ago gave up on
for the gold 85 followed by the magic of green 15.

And if, like a miracle, all of that just being there
added up to something,
I'd fall on my knees like all the winners do,
wrap myself around Drew and scream hallelujah.

But then, she comes back out, adjusts the scarf on her head, and we go pick up her kids from preschool.

Passage of the Divine Bird, Print on my Therapist's Wall

From the leather-bound chair,
she asks me if I know
when anxiety will hit.

Says "trigger" like
a horse everyone has tamed,
like I have an emotional

class schedule – morning of
ruminant thoughts, lunch
of abstract fears, strict

and separated by bells.
She says perhaps,
if we pinpoint

when it starts, then we
can get ahead of it, can
set our GPS to the specifics of

my fear of failure, defensiveness,
and just redirect, redirect,
proceed to route.

On her wall the bird, dumb
as paint, and in the chair me,
both of us scattering ourselves

above her white carpet.

There's No Easy Way to Patch

the shredded thighs on your favorite jeans,
though you wear them beyond the modesty
of underwear peeking with the rawest skin
your thighs such curved lusty things
always grabbing for each other, stealing
any touch they can, mocking the cowboy
manly canvas into lace so frail your
loose and generous seat pushes through
to its own thin sliver of air,
licking leather couch, dining chair,
grocery store freezer aisle steam.

Things Call Us to the Love of This Grief

Her eyes open to the click-flip of white numbers
in brown radio alarm clock gone dusty.

Light spills itself from the window above her bed
out across the opposite wall, frame after frame

each child with their family, fading, no photo
more recent than the last wedding thirteen years ago.

The bed groans as she slides to edge, hand on nightstand,
nearly tipping over Will's photo next to her

water glass. For a moment, she thinks her oldest
daughter visits today, she should wear the Texas

t-shirt sent at Christmas or birthday, she can't
remember. But no. That visit passed already.

Baked pork chops with green beans and
they argued at the sink about nursing homes.

Was that yesterday? Last week?
She looks out the window. Same

sky as always. Looks at the pad of paper
with rough cursive. No visitors today.

No need to dress up. She shuffles, four-pronged
walking cane to toilet and gives a happy gasp

as her tiger-striped cat chatters at her heels.

The Body of My House

To remove 100 years of roofing shingles, down to the cedar,
men not afraid to fall construct mini balance beams and lean
their full weight flat where water pools and rests above us.

From inside, it sounds like war above me, the sky falling
in waves into a red dumpster, like an open wound between
us and the neighbors who are never home, one side

swung open wide. The house shakes as nails pull free from hammers,
rust flung with black hardened from rotting boards and tar
cracked as skin gone ashy. I have felt this war before.

The pull, pull, pause. Readjust. Pull, pull. The body moving as,
beyond a curtain and the chatter of an anesthesiologist two days
from vacation, two women wrestled with my daughter,

already blue from wrapping the neck like a mid-winter scarf.
The roofers break for lunch but I avoid the kitchen, the back
window only partially obscured by the microwave.

I can feel they've been working in that corner and I've been
paralyzed to the front of the house. Too anxious to read or write.
I watch tv movie romances with awkward sex scenes,

heating up just as the dogs wake to flap open the curtains at
couch's edge while a man wearing a dark grey hoodie and drinking
Red Bull looks over to see a ridiculous blonde up against a sink

screaming "harder". It wasn't just the cord around the neck, though.
We'd rushed to the hospital because she was transverse and, in hoping
to move her just to the right head-down direction, found she had

no amniotic fluid. "But you've felt her moving, yes?"
The cord, turns out, was not only wrapped around her neck, but
also tied by some incredible gymnastic event into a true knot.

Rare, by obstetric-standards. But I never knew. I'm a twitchy
woman. Trapped on my couch by sound as roofers return,
cracking each other up to bad imitations as they shout along to

"Teen Spirit". If I leave the room for more than ten minutes, the dogs
bark incessantly. If I stay, they sleep. So I stay, hunker down for
Bridget Jones and begin to question my love of Colin Firth.

We expect at least two more days like this and I've stopped showering.
They ended up cutting three times to get her out. "War zone"
the doctor said. If we want more children, schedule them.

At the door, foreman says sorry, a hammer has been dropped,
could I go to the attic and retrieve it, please. And I go up,
through my daughter's bedroom, now a disaster as she's hit teen years.

I climb the stairs to the open ribcage of my attic, two workmen
surrounded by sky startle to see me as I hand up the hammer,
the entire body of my house, for a moment,
still as snowflakes settling mid-afternoon.

Jonie McIntire, Poet Laureate of Lucas County, Ohio (2022-2024,) is the poetry editor at *Of Rust and Glass*. *Semidomesticated* first won Red Flag Poetry's 2020 chapbook contest and was printed by Red Flag Poetry in 2021 in a limited edition of 120 copies before being reprinted by Sheila-Na-Gig Editions. Her prior chapbooks are *Beyond the Sidewalk* (Nightballet Press, 2017) and *Not All Who Are Lost Wander* (Finishing Line Press, 2016). Her poems, published in print journals, anthologies, online and even into cement, have been nominated for Best of the Net and Pushcart prizes. McIntire hosts a monthly reading series called *Uncloistered Poetry* from Toledo, Ohio. Learn about her at https://www.joniemcintire.net.

Jonie McIntire's *Semidomesticated* is looking and longing among the kitchen utensils, clearance aisles, and chemotherapy appointments that make up a life. There is so much generosity here that speaks to the daily trials we find ourselves in, as we navigate between homes and doctor's offices and jobs. How do we deal with personal loss in the face of so much being lost every day? What happens when "As if, like a miracle, all of that just being there/ added up to something,..." What happens is a pure poetic voice and a calmness of spirit—sometimes a murmur, sometimes a roar—that assuredly guides us on these journeys of a daughter, a mother, a lover, a true friend. It is a voice we can trust to give, and keep us going. It is a voice we need to be listening to.

> — **Timothy Geiger**, author of *Weatherbox*, winner of the Vern Rutsala Poetry Award (Cloudbank Books, 2019)

In *Semidomesticated*, Jonie McIntire gives us a candid glimpse inside of the everyday, making the jejune beautiful through imagery, and revealing the hidden parts with the intimacy of a close friend with a practiced eye. She also shows us the messy parts of life—anxiety, sickness, and violence—but with deftness of a thoughtful poet.

> — **DeMisty Bellinger**, author of *Peculiar Heritage* (Mason Jar Press, 2021)

www.ingramcontent.com/pod-product-compliance
Lightning Source LLC
Chambersburg PA
CBHW051650120626
46551CB00015B/2304